Copyright © 2024 Monthly Munchkins
All copyright laws and rights reserved. Published in the U.S.A.

Paperback ISBN: 978-1-63731-898-0
Hardcover ISBN: 978-1-63731-900-0
eBook ISBN: 978-1-63731-899-7

In a land of laughter under the bright sun,
Lived a munchkin named June who was always on the run.
With a giggle in her step and a twinkle in her eyes,
She dashed through adventures while eating french fries!

In June's cozy town, she loved to prance,
With her friends May and July, they'd often dance.
June had a knack for eating joyfully,
Every month had its munchkin, and June was key.

Next came Father's Day, a day for dads,
With cards, gifts, and their sketch pads,
But June got tangled in ribbons and bows,
And ended up wearing them like clothes!

Things I can do for Father's Day

1. Make a card
2. Help clean
3. Sing a song
4. Share a memory
5. Read a book together

6. Plant a flower
7. Write a poem
8. Give them a hug
9. Go for a walk
10. Take a picture together

CELEBRATE FREEDOM
JUNETEENTH

NAME

DATE

SOMETHING I LEARNED

SOMETHING ABOUT ME

www.ingramcontent.com/pod-product-compliance
Lightning Source LLC
Chambersburg PA
CBHW041714160426
43209CB00018B/1833